I0517309

Name _____

Address _____

_____

_____

_____

_____

Blank Classic

Graph Paper Notebook
            (*Geometry*)
97 numbered pages - 100 total pages
Large 8.5 x 11

Design © 2021 Blank Classic

Blank Classic

Mailing address:
Blank Classic
PO BOX 4608
Main Station Terminal
349 West Georgia Street
Vancouver, BC
Canada, V6B 4A1

Cover design by: Lauren Dick
Interior design by: Lauren Dick

ISBN: 978-1-77476-201-1

FIRST EDITION / FIRST PRINTING